designed and edited by MARTHA LONGENECKER

photography by LYNTON GARDINER

FOLK ART
OF THE SOVIET UNION
REFLECTIONS OF A RICH CULTURAL DIVERSITY OF THE FIFTEEN REPUBLICS

A MINGEI INTERNATIONAL MUSEUM DOCUMENTARY PUBLICATION

The exhibition, Folk Art of the Soviet Union, and this publication have been organized by Mingei International as a contribution to San Diego's Art Festival — Treasures of Soviet Art and Culture. Their presentation has been made possible in part by a grant from the City of San Diego and the San Diego Unified Port District.

The State Museum of Ethnography of the Peoples of the Soviet Union has generously contributed the preparation and documentation of a loan of Folk Art from its permanent collection.

The board of directors of Mingei International gratefully thanks these agencies and the many individuals who have helped to present the San Diego Arts Festival.

Special thanks are extended to the Mayor and the San Diego City Council.

Library of Congress Catalog No. 89-63305
Published by Mingei International
Museum of World Folk Art

University Towne Centre, 4405 La Jolla Village Drive
San Diego, California 92122
(mailing address: P. O. Box 553, La Jolla, CA 92038)

Copyright 1989
by Mingei International Museum

All rights reserved. Printed in the U.S.A.

ISBN #0-914155-06-7

Rarely has a community given so generously as San Diego has for its first international Arts Festival: Treasures of the Soviet Union.

This exhibition represents the most extensive display of the arts of the people of the Soviet Union ever presented in the United States.

Special thanks are due the San Diego Unified Port District for its generous funding of the exhibition, the City Council of San Diego and San Diego Arts Festival, Inc. for coordinating the Festival itself and to the Ministry of Culture of the U.S.S.R. for making this unique art and cultural program possible.

Enormous credit goes to Martha Longenecker, the Director of the Mingei International Museum of World Folk Art, for organizing this extraordinary exhibition as well as Igor Dubov, the Director of the Ethnography Museum of the People of the Soviet Union, Leningrad, and his entire staff.

So many have done so much to bring these unique works from one of the most culturally diverse nations on earth to the City of San Diego.

To each of these people, we extend our heartfelt appreciation. The Ronald McDonald Children's Charities, the James S. Copley Foundation, Helen K. Copley and Joan B. Kroc are to be forever thanked for their enlightened sponsorship.

Mayor and City Council of San Diego.

SALT CELLAR

29 x 12.5 x 26 cm

Carved wood

RUSSIA, Vologda Province
19th century

CONTENTS

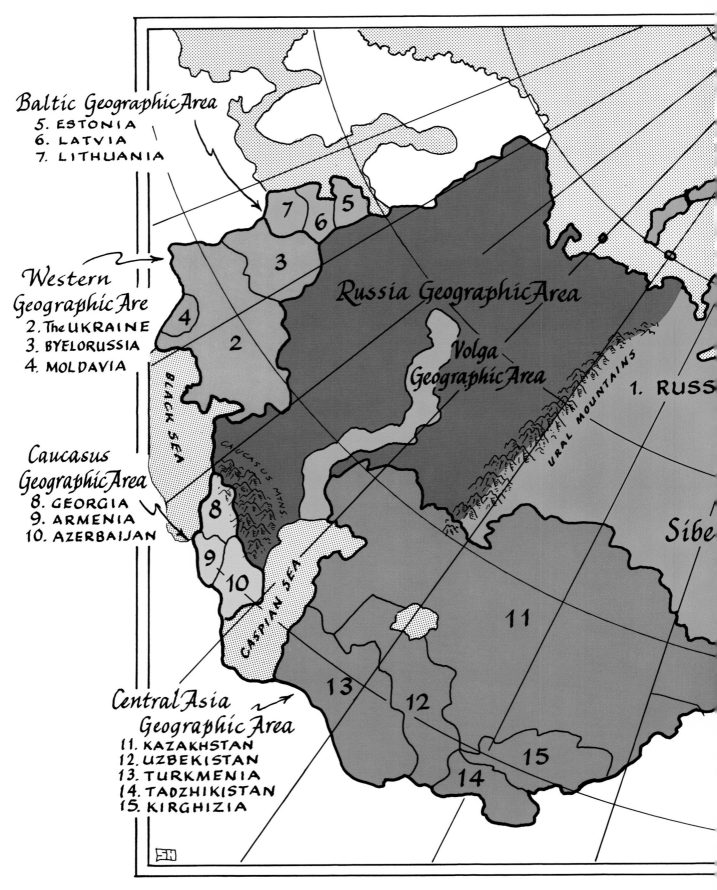

Baltic Geographic Area
5. ESTONIA
6. LATVIA
7. LITHUANIA

Western
Geographic Are
2. The UKRAINE
3. BYELORUSSIA
4. MOLDAVIA

Caucasus
Geographic Area
8. GEORGIA
9. ARMENIA
10. AZERBAIJAN

Central Asia
Geographic Area
11. KAZAKHSTAN
12. UZBEKISTAN
13. TURKMENIA
14. TADZHIKISTAN
15. KIRGHIZIA

Russia Geographic Area

Volga
Geographic Area

URAL MOUNTAINS

1. RUSS

Sibe

BLACK SEA

CAUCASUS MTNS.

CASPIAN SEA

This map indicates the boundaries and names of the fifteen
Republics of the USSR. Also shown are seven geographic areas,
three of which (Russia, the Volga, and Siberia) are within the

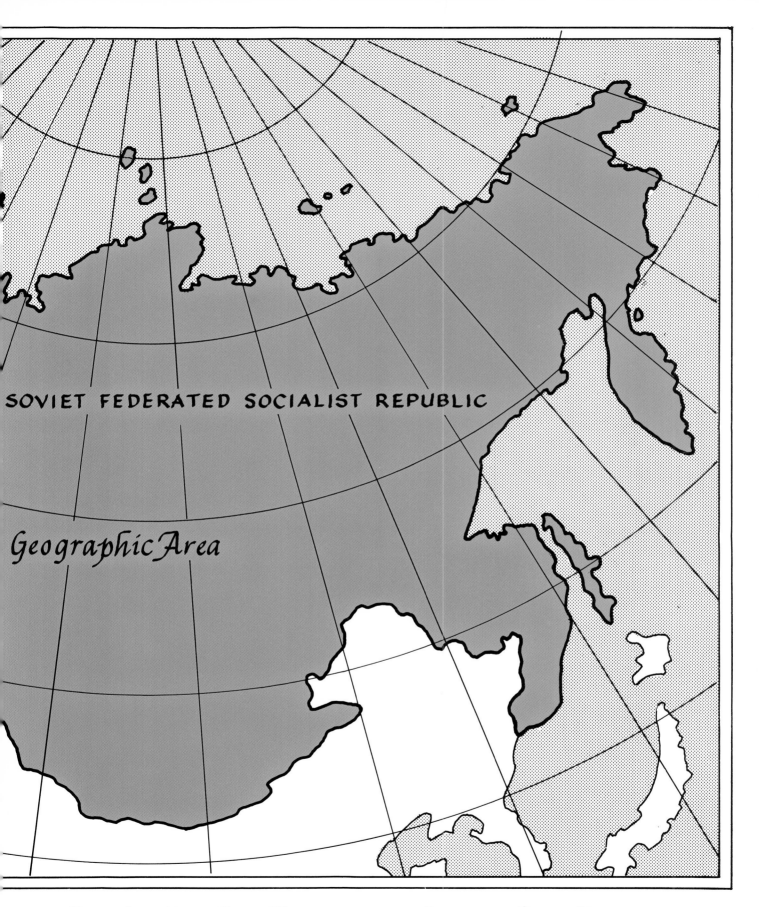

SOVIET FEDERATED SOCIALIST REPUBLIC

Geographic Area

vast Russian Republic. The remaining fourteen Republics are
grouped together to form four geographic areas ~ the Western
Area, the Baltic, the Caucasus, and Central Asia.

FOREWORD

Martha Longenecker
Director, MINGEI INTERNATIONAL MUSEUM

Here is a unique first opportunity outside of the Soviet Union to see an overview of historical and contemporary art of the people living within the vast and varied geographical areas of the Soviet Union.

This nation covers approximately one-sixth of our world's land surface, stretches from the Arctic North to the deserts of Central Asia and extends almost 7,000 miles from the European borders in the west to China and the Pacific Ocean in the east. Within this vast territory live more than one hundred different ethnic groups, each with its own language, customs, and unique cultural traditions embodied in a wide variety of art forms.

The selections were made by MINGEI INTERNATIONAL MUSEUM from the collections of one of the Soviet Union's largest museums–The State Museum of Ethnography of the Peoples of the U.S.S.R. in Leningrad. We are deeply indebted to the director of this museum and his staff including each of the geographical area's curators and researchers who so enthusiastically and skillfully prepared the exhibition.

Each object has been chosen for its aesthetic quality, crafts-manship, and regional character. All are indigenous art made by and for the people, in contrast to objects commercially produced for tourist consumption. Of unsurpassed beauty, they are used in daily life and reflect continuing changes in living traditions.

This exhibition—Folk Art of the Soviet Union—and this documentary publication are presented in the spirit of MINGEI INTERNATIONAL MUSEUM'S continuing dedication to furthering understanding of the arts of people from all parts of the world.

DOLL, "Panka"

22 cm tall
Carved wood

RUSSIA, Arkhangelsk Province
End of 18th century

11

MINGEI is a uniquely descriptive word used transculturally to represent "arts of the people." It was coined by the revered Japanese scholar, the late Dr. Soetsu Yanagi. He combined the Japanese words MIN (which means all people or everyone) and GEI (meaning art). Using this word, the movement he began is awakening people to the essential need for individuals to continue to make and use handmade objects that are unfragmented expressions of body, mind and spirit.

Utilizing the natural materials of the environment, these "arts of life"–distillations of their culture–have evolved over hundreds and thousands of years. Knowledge of materials and techniques have been passed down from father to son and mother to daughter, forming a continuity in such basic crafts as wood-working, pottery making, glass forming, weaving, dyeing, leather working, metal forming, and jewelry making.

Through the universal language of line, form, and color, these works speak directly and eloquently of the rich distinctions of individuals and the diversity of their cultural heritage. What better way is there for us to increase our understanding, respect, and admiration of all cultures of the world than through seeing and enjoying their finest and most intimate expression–the arts of the people?

cover
DUCK SHAPED BEVERAGE VESSEL

55 x 30 x 25 cm
Carved and painted wood

RUSSIA, Vologda Province
18th century

frontis page
ST. GEORGE ICON

31.5 x 27.5 cm
Painting on wood

RUSSIA
19th century

title page
DUCK SHAPED BEVERAGE VESSEL

71 x 36.5 x 25.5 cm
Carved and painted wood

RUSSIA, Yaroslavl Province
19th century

BASKET

Painted birch bark

RUSSIA

19th century

INTRODUCTION

Dr. O.A. Kondratyeva

The exhibition "Folk Arts of The Peoples of the U.S.S.R." consists
of materials from the collections of one of the Soviet Union's
largest museums—The State Museum of Ethnography of the
Peoples of the U.S.S.R.* The exhibition displays some 775
characteristic objects, dated in the 18th to 20th centuries. All
are real masterpieces of folk art, chosen to present the unique
features of the national cultures within the Soviet Union (the
Russian Empire of the pre-Revolutionary period.)

This is the first time that the Museum has sent abroad such a
large collection of rarities. The collection includes items of
different origins. Some were made by professional artisans in
large centers of artistic crafts, located near the natural sources
of raw materials, for sale in the Soviet Union and many other
parts of the world. Others were made by folk masters for local
everyday use by a limited number of people. In both categories
will be seen typical traditional pieces together with "one-of-a-
kind" masterpieces of folk art. Many materials and techniques
are present, including articles made of wood and metal, carved
ivory and ceramics, embroidery and carpets, textiles, furs and
decorated clothing.

Most products of the folk were made for daily use; house utensils, agricultural and other implements, children's toys, furniture,
musical instruments, clothes and various kinds of home
furnishings—all were made by the hands of folk masters and are
genuine creations of art. Their elegance, decorativeness and
color demonstrate the eternal striving for beauty that is
characteristic of humankind. In folk life and folk art, beauty goes
hand in hand with the useful and expedient; the harmony of
form and function is certainly one of the major characteristics of
good folk art.

Folk art cannot be regarded as a lot of unconnected individual items; it is rather a whole world of images, systems of philosophical and esthetic ideologies and spiritual experiences of a whole people. Close contact with nature, observation of the lives of plants and animals, are carried by the folk artist into the fantastic world of his dreams. Craftsmen embody in their creations a conception of ideal life, which is why so much folk art is cheerful and optimistic.

Folk art combines, in a surprisingly organic manner, antiquity and contemporaneity. Artists of every kind and in every period have gone back to folk art as a life-giving and wise source of inspiration. The study of the artistic creations of the multicultural Soviet Union is a rich source of esthetic education, an integral part of the modern human's harmonious maturity.

We must support and protect folk art. This is not less important than the guarding of natural environments; the ecology of nature and the ecology of culture are reflected in the folk art of a region, and must be nurtured and preserved as a whole.

The staff of the State Museum of Ethnography of the Peoples of the U.S.S.R. hopes that this exhibition, "Folk Arts of the Peoples of the U.S.S.R." will increase the mutual understanding between our two countries, and will bring us nearer to each other, thanks to the extremely candid, ingenuous and deeply human qualities that are embodied in folk art. For every heart responds to beauty.

SALT CELLAR

16.5 x 6 x 12 cm

Bark of linden tree, woven

RUSSIA, Vologda Province

16   19th century

*The State Museum of Ethnography of the Peoples of the U.S.S.R., like all old museums, has an interesting history—a history that is different in many respects from that of other assemblages of art in Leningrad.` The Hermitage—largest museum in the city—and the Russian Museum occupy former palaces, while the State Museum of Ethnography was designed and built as a museum. It was organized at the end of the 19th century as an Ethnographical Department of the Imperial Russian Museum, and was under the special patronage of the Tsar's family; its first director was the Grand Duke. It was decided to construct a special building, catering to the needs of both` curating the collections and placing them on display. This approach was without precedence in the pre-Revolutionary museum's practice, and demonstrates how strongly both scientists and public authorities wished to preserve and present the national cultures of the varied peoples living in Imperial Russia.

The museum now houses nearly half a million items from 153 ethnic groups of the Soviet Union, and has displays on the life and culture of forty-one of these. The basis of the museum's scientific organization is on the regional principle: the collections are compiled, stored and exhibited according to regions having a common cultural-economic structure and a common territory and history. Within each region, materials are classified according to peoples. In addition to the regional collections, the Museum has some special ones, put together on the basis of material or usage. These include the Treasury, the collection of musical instruments, the Carpet Collection and the Armoury Collection. Besides the material objects, the Museum maintains unique photographic collections and archives.

The Museum's personnel does an enormous amount of work in publishing and in setting up exhibitions; many of the latter have been sent abroad to acquaint foreign people with the rich and extremely varied culture of the peoples of our multinational country.

PADDLE
Used for beating flax or laundry

39 x 15.5 cm
Carved wood

RUSSIA, Nizhni Novgorod Province
19th century

18

RUSSIA

Galina Pluznikova

The Russians are the most numerous and widely settled people of the Soviet Union. They are also one of the largest populations of the world, numbering more than 200 million, the majority living near the European borders of the USSR. Eastward, the "strip" of solid Russian population becomes much narrower, although it does reach the Pacific coast. In Siberia and the far East, most Russians live along large rivers, in the cities, and at major seaports.

Several ethnic groups of Russians became differentiated in the mid-19th century. The largest of these groups comprised the North and South Great Russians, differing from other groups not only in appearance, but also in material and spiritual culture, in rituals, and in language. The Russian language belongs to the East Slavonic language group, which also includes Ukrainian and Byelorussian.

In the early period of historical development, the Russians, who inhabited the wooded zone of the Russian Plain, found that the nature and climate of the territory dictated their occupation— plowed agriculture. The land fed, nursed and dressed the Russian peasants. In addition to popular grains such as rye, wheat, and oats, every family also cultivated fibrous plants for weaving, raising flax in the North and hemp in the South.

The territory occupied by the Russians included much forest land; consequently, wood played an important part in the economy, and Russia has been called "Wooden Russia." The houses, bath-houses, churches, forts, utensils, housewares, sledges, carts and a host of other items were manufactured from wood.

DISTAFF
53 x 81 cm
Carved wood

RUSSIA, Vologda Province
19th century

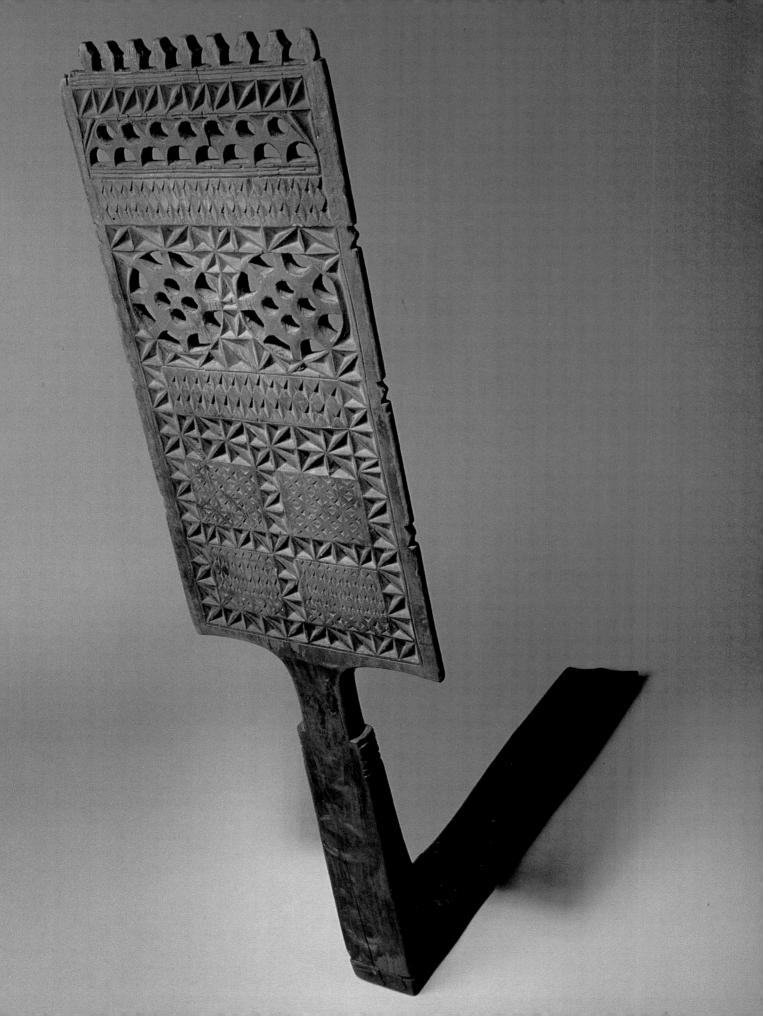

previous page
DISTAFF

57 x 85 cm

Carved and painted wood

RUSSIA, Vologda Province
1895

DISTAFF BASE

72 x 29.5 cm

Carved & painted wood

RUSSIA, Nizhni Novgorod Province
First half of 19th century

24

FISH SOUP BOWL

28 x 6 cm

Carved and painted wood

RUSSIA, Vologda Province
19th century

SPOON

18 cm long
Birch wood, painted

RUSSIA, Nizhni Novgorod Province

19th century

Cottage carpenters were not only good builders, but were also real artists. Often the peasants' houses were creations of art, with fine original carvings covering porches, gateposts, and the jambs and lintels of doors and windows. The most famous of these artists were the Volga mastercraftsmen of "ship carving." This type of carving decorated the large wooden boats that sailed up and down the great Russian river.

The design of the carved house-decks was of large scale, containing depictions of animals and birds, the most popular of which were lions and the bird Syryn; these were symbols of prosperity and joy, and were supposed to protect the house. Also popular was the river goddess, the mermaid-protector of Slavic mythology.

Not only houses, but practically all items used in everyday life, both implements and utensils, were decorated with engraving and painting. In the 18th and 19th centuries, most items were of pottery and wood; metal was rather rare in the peasants' every-day life. Wood was used for soup "shchi" bowls, big scoops, flagons, wine bowls and small dippers, flat dishes, and salt cellars.

Large cups and scoops, made from one piece of wood, were not usually carved, but rather painted with inscriptions, names of owners, and date of making. The famous center of spoon manufacturing was the Nizhni Novgorod Province. Local craftsmen produced and sold up to a half million spoons each week at the local markets; most of them were of birch or ash.

The Russian distaffs contain some of the finest decoration. Girls began spinning, using the distaff, at the age of seven, and spent

CHILD'S SLED
69 x 49 x 26 cm
Painted wood

RUSSIA, Vologda Province
19th century

SHAFT BOW
for horse's harness

112 x 81 cm
Carved and painted wood with
metal bell; with engraving
(11 cm   19th century)

NORTHERN RUSSIA
19th century

30

TOY HORSE AND SLEIGH

55 x 24 cm
Carved wood

RUSSIA, Arkhangelsk Province
End of 19th century

TOY TROIKA

82 x 19 x 29.5 cm
Carved wood

RUSSIA, Pskov Province
19th century

practically all of their youth spinning yarn. The distaff was given as a wedding gift from the bridegroom to his fiancé, or from a father to his daughter. Beautiful carved or painted distaffs were kept with care, and handed down from generation to generation. Every region of Russia had a favorite style and decor of distaffs. In the North, big distaff-spades were manufactured; in other territories, fine articles with ornate pierced carvings were made. In the Nizhegorodskaya Province they decorated not the upper part of the distaff, but the board that served as a seat for the spinner.

Other extensively decorated items in everyday life were the engraved rollers and other parts of homemade weaving looms. Of particular interest were the styles of molds used to cook spice cakes for gifts, holidays, and weddings. Over the centuries these cakes were not only the favorite delicacy of Russian children and adults, but they were also used in many ritual and religious festivities. The cake molds were usually made by professional carvers, and had rich designs representing the bird Syryn, lions, and sometimes even whole palaces.

Together with wood, the peasants used birch bark and pine tree root. These are cheap, readily available, and convenient in the making of salt cellars, boxes, bast shoes, baskets, and other items. Using different styles of wickerwork, skilled craftsmen shaped beautiful articles—utensils for gathering berries and mushrooms, and boxes with engraving and painting.

From the 10th century on, Russia perfected the skill of carving ivory, best represented by the Kholmogory productions of the 17th century. Elegant caskets, small chests and boxes were expensive, and were made for the very rich.

COVERED BASKET
in form of mug

17 x 20 cm

Pine root

RUSSIA, Kostroma Province

19th century

following page
EARTHENWARE OIL VESSEL

13 x 24 cm

Black burnished clay

RUSSIA, Yaroslavl Province
19th century

following page
BOTTLE FOR KVASS
(A Russian beverage)

12 cm top, 10.5 cm bottom x 36.5 cm
Earthenware wrapped with birch bark

RUSSIA, Tambov Province
19th century

LOVING CUP

12.5 x 15 cm

Silver, embossed, engraved with
inscription "bratina dobraya" (fine cup)

NORTHERN RUSSIA
19th century

TILED STOVE

16 x 21 cm

Clay, glazed, inscribed "the lion is running
away and the dog is attacking."

RUSSIA, Vologda Province
19th century

40

ЛѢВЪ БѢГАЕТЪ
А СОБАНА НЕ ПЕДА
ТЪ

SMALL BOX

18 x 14 x 7 cm

Ivory, wood, foil

RUSSIA, Arkhangelsk Province
18th century

CHEST

29 x 19 x 17 cm

Carved ivory, wood, foil

RUSSIA, Arkhangelsk Province
Middle 18th century

Artistic treatment of metal was less popular in Russia because of its rarity. Since old times, however, there were widespread forged, engraved or stamped vessels used as the cups of honor at feasts. There were few cast items; beautiful locks and torch standards were the most popular of these.

Pottery is one of the most ancient of the folk arts. Different Russian provinces manufactured original local forms and designs, such as the polished black ware of Yaroslavl Province. At the same time, some types of vessels, such as glazed jugs, dishes and flasks, were made everywhere. Articles in the Southern provinces typically had sculptured forms, depicting fantastic birds and animals. Together with the wares were tiles, produced for the decoration of ovens, buildings, and churches. The pictures on the tiles are extremely interesting, some of them with explanatory inscriptions.

Embroidery, a favorite occupation of women, was used for the decoration of a great many items of house furnishings and clothing. Long decorative cloth panels ("polotentse": called "rushniks" in Ukrania) were used in a wide variety of ways, especially in various rituals; brides, on the way to the church, were covered with a special polotentse.

Embroidery decorated traditional peasants' clothes, especially those used for festive occasions. The shirt received special attention. Poor people used cotton embroidery thread while the rich used threads of silk and gold. Embroidered headgear was the most treasured part of women's costumes, especially in the Northern and Central provinces, and was often passed along for generations.

DETAIL OF EMBROIDERY
OF MAN'S FESTIVE SHIRT

Linen with cotton embroidery

RUSSIA, Semipalatinsk Province

19th century

previous page
HEADDRESS

22 x 52 cm

Silk, pearl, mother-of-pearl, foil

RUSSIA, Arkhangelsk Province
19th century

previous page
HOLIDAY COSTUME
Of unmarried, rich peasant girl

Brocade, silk, cotton, linen
and mother-of-pearl

NORTHERN RUSSIA
19th century

WOMAN'S BLOUSE
Worn under a sarafan (a sleeveless tunic)

63 cm long, 69 cm sleeve
Velvet with golden embroidery

CENTRAL RUSSIA
18th century

MARRIED WOMAN'S HEADDRESS

23 x 15.5 cm

Brocade, mother-of-pearl, pearls
colored metal foil, metallic thread, colored glass

RUSSIA, Olonetz Province
19th century

HEADDRESS

26 cm high

Velvet, cotton, linen, glass,
metallic thread, spangles

RUSSIA, Kursk Province

50   19th century

HOLIDAY COSTUME

worn by young married peasant woman

Linen, wool, cotton, silk,
metallic threads, glass beads

SOUTHERN RUSSIA, Kursk Province

19th century

The festive women's headgear ("kokoshniks") were embroidered with gold and with the pearls that are found in many Northern rivers. The most popular motifs of such embroidery were birds, trees, and a woman's figure—symbols of the earth's fertility. There were often motifs of a man on horseback and a deer. Peasants' lives were closely related to nature, so floral motifs played a large role in ornamentation. Big floral designs were characteristic of the golden embroidery on silk shawls and headgear.

Women's costumes of the late 19th and early 20th centuries were greatly varied, with especially great variations among the North-Russian and South-Russian enclaves. Costumes of the Northern and Central provinces consisted of a shirt, sarafan (a sleeveless tunic), and headgear. Festive sarafans were made of brocade, damask, or taffeta. The shirt used with such a sarafan was made of a fine white textile. The costume was further embellished with a short jacket-on-straps called a "dushegreya" and headgear richly embroidered with gold and pearls. The cut of the whole outfit, with its tight upper part and broad, draping lower sarafan, emphasized the woman's figure in a magnificent, well-proportioned manner.

In Southern Russia, women did not wear the shirt and sarafan but rather a typical skirt—"ponyeva"—of ancient origin. This was made of checked domestic woolen textiles. An obligatory part of the costume was an apron which covered the whole figure in front and was usually made of ornamented textile or decorated with rich embroidery. The costumes of married women were supplemented with an ornate headgear of fine detail, completely covering the woman's hair. A characteristic feature of Southern Russian costume was its use of many colors without giving an impression of extreme brightness.

Detail
SKIRT
96 cm long
Wool, with embroidery

RUSSIA, Tambov Province
19th century

following page
BORDER
for bed cover

Cotton muslin, embroidered

RUSSIA, Nizhni Novgorod Province
19th century

THE UKRAINE, BYELORUSSIA and MOLDAVIA

Galina Pluznikova

Ukrainians, Byelorussians and Moldavians live in the west and southwest part of the European territory of the Soviet Union. The Ukrainians constitute the largest proportion of the population. These three groups of people differ in their origins; however, living close together for so long and developing similar adaptations to the common natural environment has resulted in many common features in their material and spiritual culture.

The Ukrainian and Byelorussian languages are related, and together with Russian, are included in the Slavic group of Indo-European tongues. The Moldavian language is ascribed to the East Roman group, but 40 percent of its words are Slavic.

Despite the extreme variation in natural conditions, the basic occupation is agriculture. Wheat is the main cereal, and most of it is grown in the Ukraine, the largest of the three Republics. In Byelorussia—dominated by lakes, swamps and forests, and with less fertile soil—rye, oats, and barley are the main crops. The warm climate and fertile soil of Moldavia were good for the development of viticulture and vegetable gardening.

The conditions of a semi-natural economy encouraged the development of various crafts. Many of the outstanding craftsmen live in the Ukraine. Pottery there has an ancient tradition, with each region having its own beloved traditional ornaments, patterns and coloring. Among their products were

WEATHERVANE

46 x 68 cm

Metal

UKRAINE, Chernigov Province

19th century

building ceramics, especially those used for facing stoves. The Kiev Province preferred goods with yellow, green and brown glazes, with decorations of large-scale multi-colored designs of branches, flowers, fish and birds. In Podolia, a famous center of pottery, craftsmen did not use glaze; their vessels had the natural yellow-pink coloring of the clay. For decoration they used brown clay applied in zoomorphic and anthropomorphic designs. The Chernigov ceramics were characterized by their simple undecorated forms.

From time immemorial, the Ukrainians have used embroidered towels ("rushniks") not only for house decoration but for various rituals as well. "Rushniks" accompanied peasants from birth to death, in christening, marriage, and as decoration of the grave. Another popular textile was the flat-woven carpet, with ornamentation ranging from simple geometric designs to very complicated floral ones. These carpets were used for decoration of walls, tables, trunks and beds.

The traditional men's costume of central Ukraine consisted of a domestic embroidered shirt, wide white trousers ("sharovary"), a woven belt and a broad-brimmed straw hat. Hutzuls, who lived in Western Ukrainia, were mostly shepherds and woodcutters, and had especially interesting costumes. They consisted of an embroidered shirt, bright cloth trousers, a wide leather belt, an embroidered sheepskin vest ("keptar") and a handsome cloth caftan. For holidays, Hutzuls wore a straw or felt hat decorated with flowers and feathers, and the costume was completed with a hatchet and a leather bag.

DECORATIVE CLOTH PANEL (RUSHNIK)
Used for draping icon or top of window lintel

226 x 34 cm

Linen

UKRAINE, Chernigov Province

19th century

Glass blowing arose in the Ukraine in ancient times. The masters used simple green, blue, or smoke-colored glass in the manufacture of cups, jugs, kegs, carafes and bottles, often in the shape of animals and birds. Bear-looking vessels were especially popular.

The Byelorussian peasant economy was dominated by various wood industries, which were especially important in regions with poor soil. Cottage masters used wood, bark and root to make all household utensils and containers, barrels, tubs for storing dowry and clothes, and baskets of simple and comfortable styles. Byelorussian weavers were famous for their ornamented textiles noted for their quality and whiteness, which have been traditionally used for making shirts, skirts, aprons, and other clothing for men and women. The Byelorussian costume was common throughout the whole territory. Women's clothes consisted of a linen shirt, a woolen skirt, a sleeveless jacket, and an apron. Married women followed an ancient custom by covering their heads with a complex headdress formed by folding a rushnik (a long decorative cloth panel).

The rich culture of the Byelorussian people is unique. Puppet theatres were very popular, with stages set up in the squares of towns and villages on holidays. The plays had heroic, edifying and spiritual characters. The puppets themselves were elaborate, and included representations of Kings, horsemen, the Devil, and Biblical characters.

WINE VESSEL

29 x 15 cm

Glass

UKRAINE

Early 20th century

At the end of the 19th and beginning of the 20th centuries, weaving was one of the most widespread domestic industries. Every Moldavian family manufactured all the necessary clothes and textiles for decorating their homes. Women made a lot of towels and original carpets. In the 18th and early 19th centuries, Moldavian carpets were characterized by pastel coloring. Beginning in the mid-19th century, they changed to black, brown and red coloring, with roses as the favored pattern. In addition to large wool carpets, there were woolen runners, used to decorate floors, benches, and walls. A lot of these went into guest rooms, where much of the best family property was kept. It was also there that the bride usually dressed before the marriage. The costume of the Moldavian bride was reserved in coloring, and consisted of a shirt with embroidered sleeves and a black sarafan with dark velvet ribbons sewn on the hem. The costume was vivified with a woven belt with ribbons, and a bright gala garland.

SUEDE JACKET

Suede, leather applique, fur lined
and embroidered

UKRAINE
Early 20th century

EARTHENWARE VESSEL

14 cm base, 24 cm neck x 23 cm
Unglazed terra cotta with iron brush decoration

EARTHENWARE JUG

8.5 cm base, 11 cm neck x 31 cm
Unglazed earthenware

UKRAINE, Poltava Province

19th century

SERVING BOWL

17 x 4.5 cm

Lead glazed earthenware, brush decoration

UKRAINE, Podolsk Province
Early 20th century

TILE

16 x 19.5 cm

Glazed terracotta

UKRAINE

19th century

BASKET

41 x 20.5 cm

Willow

BYELO RUSSIA, Grodno Region

68   1950's

PITCHERS

Largest 35 cm high

Lead glazed earthenware, copper green

BYELO RUSSIA

Contemporary

DECORATIVE CLOTH PANEL
*Used in interior of home for
draping religious icon or window*

Linen, beige and white double weave

BYELO RUSSIA, Brest Region

70   1976

DECORATIVE CLOTH PANEL
*Used in interior of home for
draping religious icon or window*

100 x 51 cm
Linen, with sequins

MOLDAVIA, Bukovina area

DECORATIVE CLOTH PANEL
*Used in interior of home for
draping religious icon or window*

364 x 55 cm

Linen

MOLDAVIA, Kishinev Region

Early 20th Century

BALTIC

M. Zasetskaya

On rainy windy days, the waves of the Baltic Sea seem heavy as lead. Bleak is the gray sky, gloomy are the rocks and forest. But the first rays of the sun change the scene; raindrops become small diamonds, and hundreds of rainbows crown the old gray boulders, the high pine and fir trees.

The sun is not the only force that determines the nature of the Baltic Region. Another is the character of the people who live in this severe land. They are tireless toilers, masters of all trades, and their inspired musicians and bards make music so that, as in other folk cultures, labor and song are indivisible.

The Eastern Baltic area is inhabited by the Estonians, Lithuanians, and Letts, each of which has its own separate Republic— Estonia, Lithuania, and Latvia.

Estonians, who speak a language of the Ural-Altaic family, are descended from the ancient Finno-Ugric tribes that migrated to the Baltic coast in the 3rd or 4th millenium B.C. Their closest relatives are the Finns and Hungarians along with the Mordvin people, Udmurts and other people from the Volga region.

The Lithuanians and Letts are direct descendants of ancient Baltic tribes who came from the south in the 2nd millenium B.C. The languages of the Lithuanians and Letts comprise the Baltic group of the Indo-European language family.

Despite their different origins, all three of these populations share many common features of economics, culture and history. By the early medieval period, they had already formed the basic economy of farming and fishing, which prevailed to the 19th century.

FLAXHOLDER
Mounting for top of spinning wheel

12 x 27 cm
Carved wood

BALTIC, Lithuania
End of 19th century

74

Long ago, seafaring developed into both trade and piracy. Using boats similar to those of the Vikings, Baltic warriors sailed on the wild sea as far as Scandinavia. They feared only the "Finnish wizards" who were said to be the "Rulers of the Wind."

Unlike their eastern neighbors, the Russians, the Baltic people adopted Christianity very late; the Letts, converting in the 14th century, were the last Europeans to do so. Accepting the Roman Catholic religion, the Baltic culture was oriented more to Western Europe than to the east.

A tragic period in Baltic history began in the 12th century, when Germans and Danes conquered the area. The history of the Baltic was bloody and full of suffering, with parts of the territory being yielded to one invader after another. In the 18th century Peter the Great conquered the eastern coast of the Baltic Sea. With all this, an interesting and enduring form of "folk" or "peasant" life prevailed until the mid-19th century.

All traditional folk art is linked in some way to the production of useful articles. An old Lithuanian proverb says, "Don't ask a Lithuanian for a talkative speech or a cheerful song, but ask him to show his mastership in wood-carving."

The same can be said of all the Baltic people, who are great masters of woodworking. The most beautiful and detailed pieces—distaffs, boxes, and tankards—are given to brides.

A traditional wedding was not only a holiday, but a test as well, especially for the bride; "A good daughter-in-law will clothe her

TANKARD

16.5 x 26 cm

Carved wood

BALTIC, Estonia

Second half of 19th century

WOMAN'S HAT

22 cm high
Linen with wool, embroidered

BALTIC, Estonia
Second half of 19th century

WOMAN'S COSTUME

Wool, linen and metal

BALTIC, Estonia (Saarema Island)
Mid 19th century

mother-in-law from head to foot." The bride had to demonstrate her skills by presenting gloves, stockings, and a belt to every relative of her future husband. The wife or mistress of every Baltic peasant says:

> "Stove stoking, stocking knitting;
> In the twilight, plaiting belt,
> And the mittens decorated
> In the first light of the dawn."

The distinctiveness of Baltic costume lay in its variation; in the early 20th century there were nearly 160 different types in Estonia. Clothes could define, among other things, a person's origin, family ties, social status, and age. One of the most unusual costumes is that of the women from Saaremaa Island. Their cut, color, lace, embroidery, headgear and silver decorations provide a fine example of folk costumes, exemplifying craftsmanship and esthetic design in the highest degree.

The meaning of folk costume and traditional crafts has not been lost in today's culture, but has formed the basis for contemporary design, sculpture, painting, and applied arts in clay, fiber, wood and metal.

Baltic pottery-making flourished in the 19th century, and in 1905, Drynda, one of the most talented master potters, was awarded first prize for ceramics in the Paris Exhibition.

Many traditional items have symbolic meanings. For example, the gift of a wooden shoe means "come again to see us," and amber beads mean "I love you."

GLAZED EARTHENWARE

30 cm diameter
Lead glazed earthenware

BALTIC, Latvia
Early 20th century

VOLGA

A.Y. Zadnaprovakaya

The Volga is a special geographic and cultural region of eastern Europe. The core of its unification is the presence of the great and magnificent rivers, the Volga and the Kama, which were the primary means of transportation. Traveling along these rivers, one can see distinctly the variety in both nature (from northern taiga to Caspian semi-desert) and human culture. Along these rivers and their many tributaries live many Russian people of the Finno-Ugric groups: Komi, Udmurts, Mari, Mordovians and Turkic-speaking Chuvash, Tatars and Bashkirs.

Agriculture is the main occupation of these people. They cultivate crops such as rye and wheat as basic foods. The most abundant non-food crop is hemp, which produces fiber used in textiles.

The culture of the Volga region can justly be called "wooden." Wood is used for all things necessary to life; household goods, furniture, implements, utensils, and footwear are made from many different kinds of wood; pine, fir and linden are especially popular, along with bast (the inner bark of the linden tree) and birch bark.

The soul of the nation and its concept of beauty is most vividly represented in the various types of women's art. In this region the most impressive are ornamented textiles, embroidery and beads. The most praiseworthy activity of the peasant bride is her skill in making clothes. At the wedding there are organized exhibitions of clothing, one of the main components of the dowry, and they are scrutinized by all the guests.

BEER LADLE

34 x 16 cm

Wood

VOLGA REGION, Chuvash

Mid 19th century

83

Volga costumes are complicated in structure, and are bright and multi-colored. The core of the costume is a hempen tunic-cut dress with a sarafan, apron, belt, and complex headdress. The whole outfit is decorated with bright, original geometric embroidery, which is done with no advance drawing. The embroidery threads are of silk and wool, colored with natural vegetable dyes. Synthetic dyes were not introduced into the Volga region until the early 20th century.

The costumes have a woven belt, along with a whole set of pendants, tassels, and embroidered cloths; abundant decoration is obligatory. These decorations, mostly homemade, are made of coins, beads and shells. Many of them function as amulets designed to ward off the evil eye and to promote the health and happiness of the wearer.

Headdresses and other decorations, often used with birth, wedding and funeral ceremonies, are designed to depict the wearer's family line and age status.

The spiritual culture of the Volga people combines ancient pagan beliefs and Christianity. Orthodoxy, the official church of Russia, came to the Volga region in the 17th and 18th centuries. In the 18th and 19th centuries, the area was the scene of competition between Christianity and Islam. The Islamic religion is traditional with the Tatars and Bashkirs. These spiritual values and the original traditions of the culture of the Volga region are reflected in the arts of the people.

HIP DECORATION
50 x 27 cm
Wool, metal, beads

VOLGA REGION, Mordvin
End of 19th century

CHEST ORNAMENTS

28 x 11 cm
Metal, beads, glass

34 x 16 cm
Beads, metal, glass

VOLGA REGION, Mordvin
Second half of 19th century

KERCHIEF

123 x 80 cm
Linen, silk

VOLGA REGION, Mari
Late 19th century

previous page
KERCHIEF OF GROOM
47 x 36 cm
Linen, silk

VOLGA REGION, Chuvash
Mid 19th century

Detail
CHEST EMBROIDERY
34 x 25 cm
Linen, silk

VOLGA REGION, Chuvash
Mid 19th century

92

following page
SLEEVE EMBROIDERY

54 x 22 cm

Textile, gold and silver threads

VOLGA REGION, Udmurt
End of 19th century

following page
CRADLE COVER

158 x 106 cm

Flax, cotton

VOLGA REGION, Udmurt
Beginning of 20th century

HAT

47 x 22 cm

Metal, wood, gold thread, textile

VOLGA REGION, Mordvin
Second half of 19th century

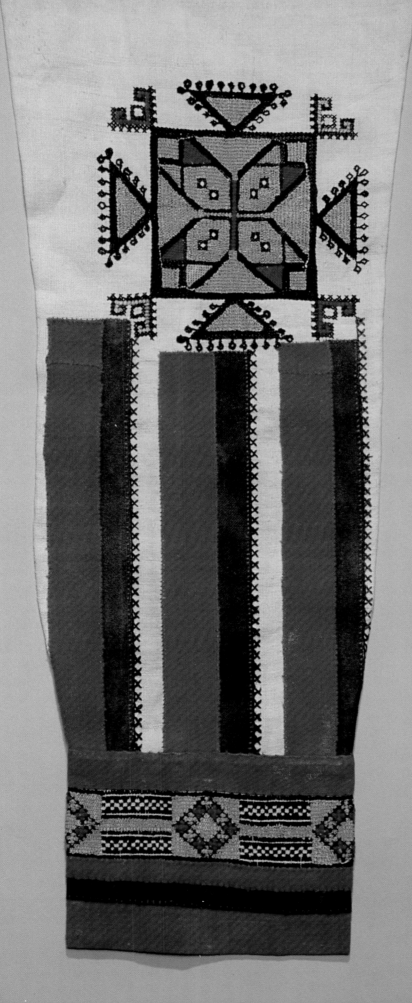

HEADDRESSES

26 x 43 cm

Textile, beads, golden threads

30 x 26 cm

98   Velvet, metal thread, black and gold embroidery

VOLGA REGION, Tatars

Early 20th century

CAUCASUS

Dr. V.A. Dmitriyev

The Caucasus area is often called the "bridge between Europe and Asia." This relatively narrow strip of land extends between the Black and Caspian Seas, and its east-west mountain ranges divide the world of the South Russian steppes from the Near East. All immigrants from Eurasia necessarily passed through the Caucasus and some inevitably settled in the mountains.

This geographical area consists of such contrasting regions as highlands, fertile valleys, luxurious subtropical regions on the Black Sea and dry semi-deserts on the Caspian. This variety in its land has contributed to the complexity of its civilization.

It was in the southern part of the Caucasus territory that some of humanity's basic occupations began: agriculture, cattle breeding, and crafts production. Not without reason the Bible legends place Eden, the earthly paradise, in the Caucasus, and Noah's Ark landed here after the Flood. Well known ancient Persian legends testify to the richness of the Caucasian lands, as does the Hellenic epos of the Argonauts, who sailed to the Eastern coast of the Black Sea in search of the Golden Fleece.

The long and dramatic history of the Caucasus tells of many conquerors who came to find treasures and left behind the ruins of cities and villages. Foreign invasion stopped only after the first half of the 19th century, when the Caucasus became part of Russia. Evidence of the stormy events of the past is seen in ancient and medieval fortresses and the villages and houses of the highlanders. There is further testimony in the great number of Caucasians all over the world, with their love of weaponry and admiration for the hero-warrior.

COVER FOR PILAF DISH

28 x 24 cm

Copper

CAUCASUS, Azerbaijanian
End of 19th century

previous page
WINE VESSEL

25 cm high
Coconut, silver engraving

CAUCASUS, Georgian
End of 19th century

previous page
WINE VESSEL

30 cm high
Silver

WOMAN'S COSTUME

Velvet, cotton, silk

CAUCASUS, Armenian
End of 19th century

The process of forming the Caucasian population was complex and varied. The Trans-Caucasus became the center of origin of three populations, Georgians, Armenians, and Azerbaijanians, each with a history of past separate nationhood. Topographic and historical conditions made Georgia and Armenia the outpost of the east-Christian world in Asia. The unique script and traditions of this language-cultural community were developed early. The people of Azerbaijan represent a blending of primordial Caucasian, Iranian and Turkic roots. The Islamic Shiite sect promoted the strengthening of Azerbaijan-Persian contacts.

The Daghestan area, on the northern and southern slopes of the main Caucasus range, has an abundance of isolated ravines which make travel very difficult, and have promoted the development of individual ethnic groups. This has helped to keep family and social life fairly static over many generations. There are many isolated groups of people, many with their own languages. It is not by accident that Daghestan, with its nearly 30 ethnic groups, has been called both "the country of mountains" and "the mountain of languages."

In the past, the populations of Daghestan and the Northern Caucasus have adhered mainly to the Sunnite sect of Islam, along with a good many "heathen" cults. Some of the Ossetians, living in the central parts of the Northern Caucasus, have followed the Greek Orthodox church. The mixture of Christian and Moslem traditions with ancient folk practices has resulted in a syncretism in folk architecture, costume, houses, utensils and verbal folklore.

Many peculiarities of economy and everyday life have ancient roots, and are held in common throughout most of the

MAT

312 x 135 cm

Wool, grass fiber

CAUCASUS, Dagestan: Avars

End of 19th century

Caucasus. Among them is the honoring of the labor of peasants and wine-growers, the leading role of sheep breeding in the economy, the well-defined divisions between the activities of men and women, highly developed crafts, the authoritative position of the elderly, and passionate patriotism. Such shared features are combined with an abundance of unique local peculiarities.

Such a combination is seen especially in the costumes. One of the most basic styles of male attire was developed in the northern Caucasus and spread everywhere; the style combines the image of a rider and a warrior, and weapons form a traditional part of the costume. Women's clothes, while varied, had one common feature arising from different prohibitions, requiring the hiding of the hair, the lower part of the face, and hands and feet. The items thus used also denoted the status of the woman's family. Women's costumes are noted for the amulets and symbols, made of jewelry and silver, colored insets and embroidery, all designed to ward off evil spirits. Silver was also used in men's costumes, especially on the weapons.

Ancient mythology recognizes the role of the Caucasus as a center for the crafts. Among the most numerous craftspeople were blacksmiths, silversmiths, armorers, jewelers, carpet weavers, potters, and manufacturers of silk textiles and printed cloth. Treatment of metal, stone, and wood were the province of men, while carpet making fell to the women. Both women (in Armenia and Daghestan) and men (in Daghestan, Georgia, Armenia and Azerbaijan) worked in pottery.

WALL HANGING

Fabric

Dagestan: Kaitag

End of 19th century

The main centers of crafts included Tbilisi, Baku, Alexandropol and Elisavetpol, as well as some villages in Daghestan and the Trans-Caucasus, of which Kubachi was the most famous. In Daghestan, there were many villages, each of which specialized in a particular craft. Among the crafts people there were many seasonal workers, and many doing commissioned work. Caucasian weapons, jewelry and rugs were always popular in Asian and European markets.

The cultural heritage of the Caucasus is very valuable and attracts researchers of many different orientations, and always arouses admiration.

previous page
SALT CELLARS
26 cm
Wood

CAUCASUS, Dagestan
End of 19th century

BAG FOR SALT
57 x 42 cm
Wool

CAUCASUS, Armenian
End of 19th century

following page
HORSE COVER
196 x 133 cm
Wool

CAUCASUS, Azerbaijanian

End of 19th century

CENTRAL ASIA

Elena Georgieva Tsareva

The Central Asia and Kazakhstan region is one of the U.S.S.R.'s largest, second only to Siberia. Because of its climate and altitude, this geographical region is one of extremes. Within its territory are found the vast hot deserts that contrast with the highest and coldest mountain peaks in the country. In the sunny Central Asian lowlands on a summer day, the sun beats down like a waterfall; in the Pamir mountains on that same day, one could play with snowballs.

The inhabitants of Central Asia share some features in common, such as dark hair, dark eyes, and thick sunburnt skin, giving them a similar appearance despite their different origins. Some, like the Tajiks and Turkmen, are descended from European Stock, while others, like the Kirghiz, Kazakhs, Karakalpaks and Uzbeks, belong to the Mongolian race. The only exception in coloring is that of the Pamir Mountain Tajiks, many of whom have blue or gray eyes, light skin and light hair; they are the descendants of Iranian nomads who arrived in the 2nd millenium B.C. and established a rich and interesting culture based on the steppes and oasis towns. These groups were tightly linked by political, cultural, and trade contacts in a system that was characteristic of the region up to the 20th century.

Once a part of the great Akhemenian empire, Central Asia lived through the invasion of Alexander the Great, who was so charmed by the land and its people that he made Central Asia an important part of his state, and even married a local princess named Roksana. Survivals of Greek-Bakhtrian culture can be traced to the present day, especially in decorative design and jewelry. The jewelry of Turkmen and Karakalpak women still seems inspired by warriors' raiment, making plausible the Greek stories of women-warriors, the "Amazons."

VESSEL FOR MILK

45 x 27 cm

Leather, wood

CENTRAL ASIA, Kirghiz

Second half of 19th century

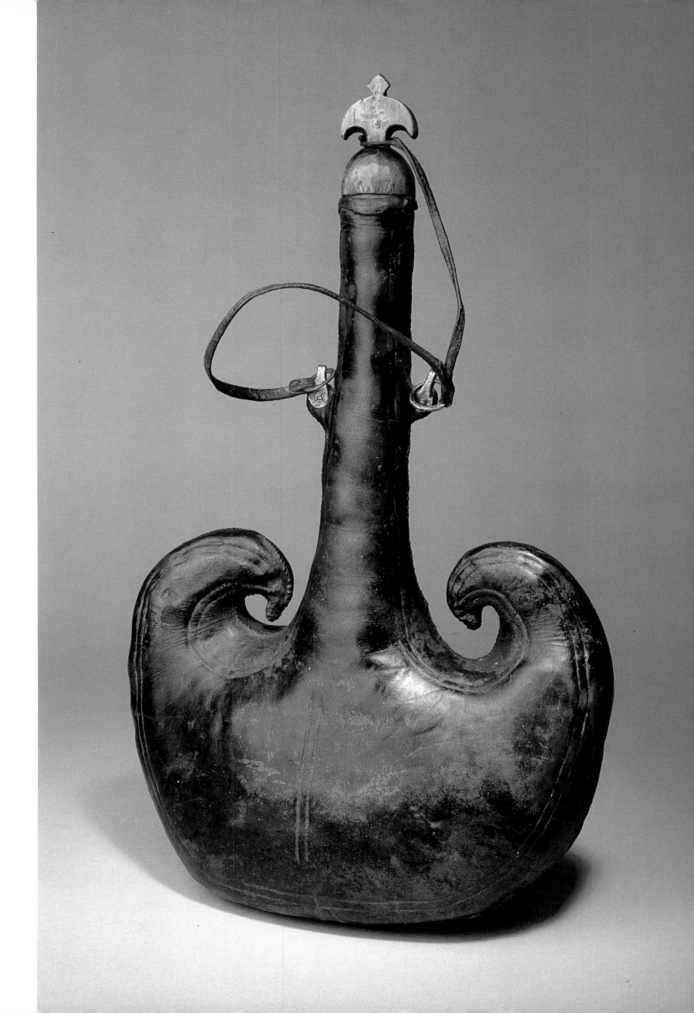

One of the most important elements in the defining of the Central Asia culture was the Great Silk Road, which passed through at least half of the territory over a period of nearly three millenia. Positioned on the world's crossroads, Central Asia was subject to numerous invasions. These resulted in great hardships for the people, but at the same time they enriched the local culture which collected, like a vessel containing an ancient magic potion, precious drops left by the newcomers.

Alexander the Great was the only conqueror who came from the West. Others, like the Arabs, came from the South, but most were from the East. All serious invasions by such Turkic tribes as Huns and Mongols (some of whom advanced as far as Europe) passed through Central Asia. In passing, they partly destroyed and partly adopted the rich local culture. Being breeders of cattle and sheep, the invaders preserved the nomadic way of life, although some of the Uzbeks settled in the oases and became part of the Tajiks. Both the nomadic and the settled lifestyles are still traditional in Central Asia.

The nomads live in a tent called a "yurt" or a "kibitka" which can be easily dismantled to accommodate the demands of constant travel. The yurt frame consists of latticed walls and poles that curve upward to support a domed roof of felt. The furnishings are carpets, felts, and various bags for holding clothes and utensils. The construction and furnishing of the yurt are ideal for the nomadic way of life, and were developed over the course of many generations.

LADLE FOR KOUMISS
(Fermented mare's milk)

62 x 17 cm

Wood

CENTRAL ASIA, Kirghiz

Late 19th century

119

The nomads, particularly the Turkmen, are superior in the making of carpets, felts, leather goods and wooden items. Other easily transported objects, such as jewelry and embroidery, were also very well developed. The crafts of producing such objects were passed from mother to daughter, from father to son, from generation to generation. This tradition was one of the main reasons for Central Asia's esthetic development and cultural continuity. The quality of Central Asian art is a result of the high levels of skill and sensitivity attained through generations of practice. At an early age children are introduced to the charm of craftsmanship beginning with easy tasks; they become skilled masters only after 20 years or so. The arts of these people are usually anonymous, and it is often difficult to distinguish articles made in the 17th century from those of the 19th.

The settled populations of the oases—Tajiks, Uzbeks and Turkmen—follow a way of life that differs distinctly from that of the nomads, but nevertheless shares many features of the common local culture. The main occupations of this settled population are gardening and large-scale agriculture, both requiring irrigation.

Large cultural, economic, and administrative centers such as Bukhara and Samarkand are world renowned for their crafts. They fulfill both local needs and demands from abroad, mainly from the Orient and other parts of the Soviet Union. The Bukharian and Samarkand copper items, textiles (especially silk and velvet), ceramics and embroidery on silk or wool were also highly valued.

TENT BAG "CHUVAL"
For clothes storage

135 x 100 cm

Wool, silk, cotton

CENTRAL ASIA, Turkmen, Saryks

Mid 19th century

CAMEL TRAPPING
For wedding ceremony

162 x 92 cm

Wool

CENTRAL ASIA, Turkmen, Tekes

18th century

After 1860, Central Asian objects of art became popular in St. Petersburg. The most luxurious items—embroidery in gold and silver, rich cold steel, jewelry, embroidered hangings and carpets—were used by Central Asian authorities as gifts to the Russian Tsar's family.

A characteristic of this traditional culture is the richness of its color and ornamentation of its decorations. In Central Asia there are many magic symbols, used especially in children's costumes and objects for wedding ceremonies. Some designs, such as ram's horns, symbolize prosperity and can be traced back to the Stone Ages. Every valley, every tribe, had its own unique design. Some decorations, such as the octagonal "gul" design on Turkmen carpets, had the significance of a tribal coat of arms.

The making of many objects was accompanied by particular rituals evolved over many centuries. Some beliefs concerning the production of articles were known only to the craftsmen, while others were widely understood. The finest and most refined pieces were deliberately left with some minor incompletion, as it was felt that perfection is the prerogative only of God.

DOOR SURROUNDING

87 x 119 cm

Wool, cotton

CENTRAL ASIA, Turkmen, Saryks

Early 19th century

125

TENT BAND

12 cm wide
Wool

CENTRAL ASIA, Kirghiz
Early 20th century

SAMPLE OF VELVET TEXTILE

218 x 33 cm
Velvet

CENTRAL ASIA, Tajiks-Uzbeks
126 Late 19th century

Bukhara was famous not only for its crafts, but was the most important Central Asian center of education and religion. Islam, introduced by the Arabs in the 8th Century, greatly influenced the cultural life of the region. Many ancient genres, however, flourished independently of Mohammedanism or even in spite of it. The traditional musical culture, theatre, holiday rituals, fine arts, miniatures, mosaics, schematized human figures—all survived despite Islamic disapproval. Survivals of pre-Islamic belief are found even in contemporary art such as ceramic dragons and fantastic birds and animals.

The Central Asian culture is so colorful that even when removed from the context of their natural surroundings, the arts of the people charm us. The variety of forms, decorations, materials and colors shown here represent just a shadow of the unforgettable richness and beauty of the region that is Central Asia.

BRAID BACK ORNAMENT

17.5 x 27 cm

Silver, carnelian, camel hair

CENTRAL ASIA, Turkmen

19th century

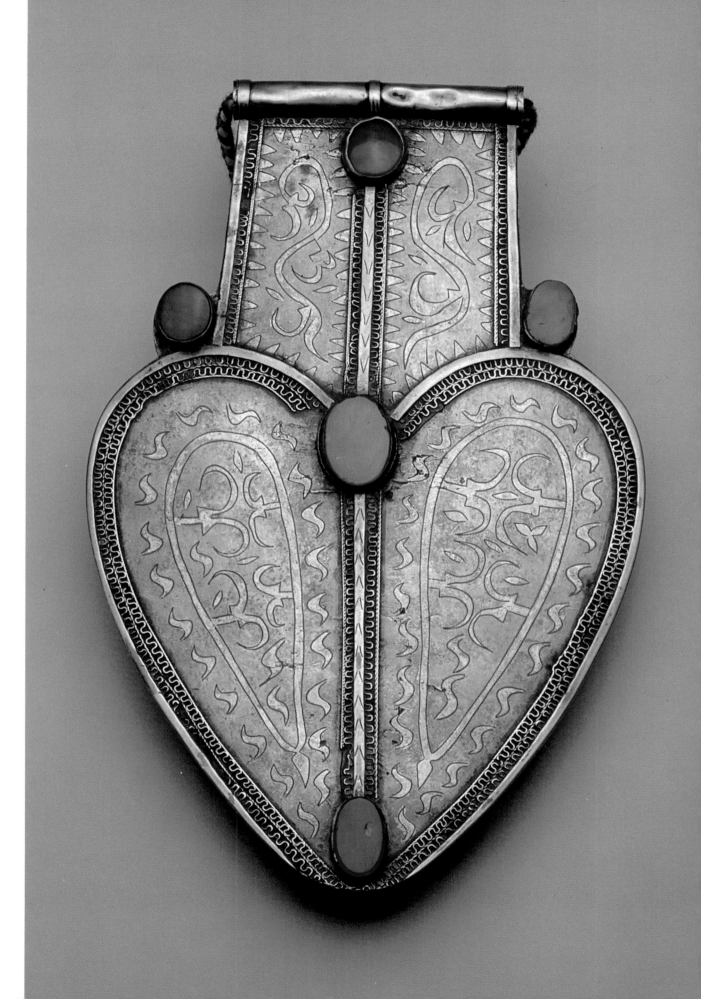

WOMAN'S PURSE

56 (with belt) x 9.5 (case) x 12 cm

Leather, silver, cornelian

CENTRAL ASIA, Turkmen

130   18th, early 19th century

TEMPLE RINGS

15 x 2.5 cm
Silver, coral, enamel, human hair

DIADEM — FOREHEAD ORNAMENT

26 x 17 cm
Silver, gilding enamel, glass

CENTRAL ASIA, Bukhara, Tajiks

19th century

WOMAN'S COSTUME

Silk

134   CENTRAL ASIA, Tajik, Bukhara

135

GROOM'S HANDKERCHIEF

78 x 36 cm
Cotton, silk threads

BRIDE'S VEIL

74 x 55.5 cm
Cotton, silk threads

CENTRAL ASIA, Mountain Tajiks
18th century

136

ROBE OF HIGH RANKING OFFICIAL

138 cm high
Silk, gold threads

CENTRAL ASIA, Bukhara, Tajiks
Late 19th century

HORSE TRAPPING

194 (bottom), 123 (top) x 153 (with fringe) cm
Silk textile, gold and silver threads

CENTRAL ASIA, Bukhara, Tajiks
Second half of 19th century

140

BRIDAL HEADDRESS

Tail: 162 cm   Cap: 31 x 20 cm
Gold, pearls, coral, carnelian, cotton, wool, silk threads

CENTRAL ASIA, Karakalpaks
142   18th century

previous page
CHILD'S ROBE

45.5 x 54 cm

Silk, cotton, metal, hair

CENTRAL ASIA, Turkmen
19th century

previous page
MAN'S TROUSERS
(Fragment)

Suede, silk threads

CENTRAL ASIA
Late 19th century

WALL HANGING

170 x 231 cm
Cotton, silk threads (embroidery)

CENTRAL ASIA, Tajiks
19th century

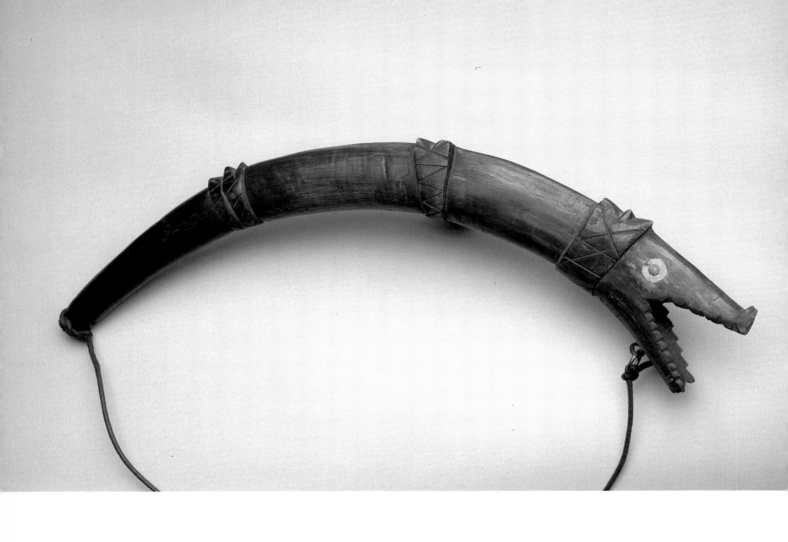

HORN
Musical instrument

58.5 cm long
Wood, paint, leather

CENTRAL ASIA, Tajiks
Late 18th century

STRINGED MUSICAL INSTRUMENT

76 x 17 cm
Wood, metal, veins, cotton

CENTRAL ASIA, Mountain Tajiks
148 Early 18th, 19th century

SIBERIA

K.Y. Soloujeva

From the Ural range in the west to the Pacific Ocean in the east, from the Arctic Ocean in the north to the borders of China and Mongolia in the south, stretches the vast territory known all over the world as Siberia.

For many people, Siberia is known only for its hard, severe climate with enormous icy plains, impassable snows and nights lasting half a year. All of this is true—but there is much more. The boundless tundra, with its multitude of shallow lakes, is replaced to the south by the Siberian taiga, containing thousands of square miles with numerous conifers and such deep, powerful rivers as the Lena, Ob, Irtysh, Kolyma, Enisey and Amur.

In the south, landscapes of mountain and forest are dominant. From time immemorial, this fabulously wealthy country has been inhabited by the indigenous peoples of Siberia and the Far East. These include about 30 ethnic groups. A few of these are: Khanty, Mansi, and Nentsy in Western Siberia; Chuktchi, Koryaks and Eskimo in the Northeast; Nivkhs, Nanay, Ultchi, Orotchi and Udeghe in the Far East; Evenks and Evens in East Siberia; Yakuts and Buryats in East and South Siberia. Altogether, they total a little over a million people. The largest population is that of the Yakuts (328,000); then come the Buryats (353,000), Chuktchi (14,000), Khanty (21,000) and on down to the smallest; Udeghe (1,600), Eskimo (1,500) and Neghidals (500).

Natural conditions can't be separated from the lives of indigenous people, and they define the people's occupations, ways of life, and culture. The main occupations of the local people are reindeer herding in the North, hunting and fishing in the taiga region, fishing and whaling in the Northeast, and cattle breeding in the South. These occupations define lifestyles, nomadic in the North and South, and semi-nomadic and settled in the taiga.

"CHORON" VESSEL FOR KOUMISS
(Fermented mare's milk)

16 x 21 cm
Wood

SIBERIA, Yakut
19th century

the taiga region, fishing and whaling in the Northeast, and cattle breeding in the South. These occupations define lifestyles, nomadic in the North and South, and semi-nomadic and settled in the taiga.

In the domestic economy of the 19th and 20th centuries, the necessities of life were produced by the family for itself. Most work was assigned either to men or women. Men worked wood and ivory, and made objects necessary for life and work. Women prepared food, gathered berries and mushrooms, processed skins, and made clothing. Women also stored birch-bark, using it to make utensils and other everyday objects, and they were responsible for keeping house and raising children.

The peoples of Siberia and the Far East are different in language, culture, and anthropological types. Still, because there are no fixed ethnic borders, extensive cultural interpenetration has taken place. Through many centuries there have been constant economic and cultural contacts between the northern and southern territories of Siberia and the ancient civilizations of East and West. Precious northern furs reached not only the Chinese market, but those of Central Asia and India as well. There were cultural links between Western Siberia and Eastern Europe. Yet, despite these interactions, every population has its own bright and indigenous art exemplifying its concepts of the surrounding world, the richness and color of nature, and the feelings of rhythm, beauty and inexhaustible fantasy of the folk masters.

IDOL
(Guardian of house)

79 cm high
Wood

SIBERIA, Nanai
19th century

COVERED BOX

18 x 27 cm
Birch bark, wood

SPOON HOLDER

30 x 13 cm
Birch bark, wood

SIBERIA, Ulchi
154   End of 19th century

LADLE FOR KOUMISS
(Fermented mare's milk)

83 x 19 cm
Wood

COVERED BOX

14 x 16 cm
Wood, birch bark, beads, horse's hair

SIBERIA, Yakut
156   19th century

The earliest of the decorative pieces for ceremony and for daily use can be traced to the middle and second half of the 19th century. Everything was produced at home, as professional art did not appear until the 20th century.

The costumes of Siberia and the Far East are appropriate to the severe climate. They are made from the skins of various animals and decorated with striped textiles, fur mosaics, beads and embroidery. Girls begin practicing the art of making clothes at a very early age. They are taught the difficult art of choosing materials by studying the length of the fur, and its softness, color and quality. In the North, clothing is decorated with reindeer neck hair, reindeer leather strips, colored seal hair, and strips of leather made from the neck skin of dogs and seals. Among the Nanaiis, Ultchi, and Nivkhs on the banks of the Amur, fish skins were also used in the making of clothes, hats, shoes, sails, utensils and bags. The people of the Amur are very knowledgeable about the qualities of various types of fish skins, some of which are durable and waterproof, and can be used for raincoats. Some were richly colored with vegetable dyes and used for special festive occasions, as were men's and women's textile robes, decorated with embroidery and applique work.

One of the most popular materials was birch-bark, especially in the taiga region, where it had a wide variety of uses. This bark was treated with high temperatures, and was long-lasting because of its resistance to sun and water. Birch-bark utensils were richly decorated with engravings, paintings, and carvings; the Yakuts often decorated with horsehair and beads. They, and the people living along the Amur River, were the most skilled in birch-bark craft.

WOMAN'S DRESSING GOWN

109 cm high

Fish skin, painted

SIBERIA, Nanai

Beginning of 20th century

The production of wooden objects is a man's occupation. Many interesting items were made for special occasions. For example, the artistic tastes and ideas of the Yakuts are brightly reflected in the staging of the spring holiday "Ysakh"—the celebration of nature's rebirth after the cold winter. It was connected with the cult of the horse. During the ritual koumiss-drinking—an obligatory part of the holiday—special vessels were used, such as large ladles, and cask-shaped "chorons" carved from solid wood. The Amur people used many wood objects for family and tribal occasions—large scoops, dishes and spoons produced by the best masters.

The spiritual life of the Siberian and Far Eastern people is rich and original, preserving many archaic beliefs. Shamanism, the personal embodiment of spiritual ideas, was widespread. The priests (shamans) of this cult were regarded as intermediaries between people and the spirits. A shaman's purpose was to protect his people from evil spirits, to help them in worldly affairs, and to engage in fortune-telling and prophecy. His power was magnified by his clothing, which was covered with many iron pendants; his crown was decorated with the depiction of a reindeer's antlers, symbolizing the unity of bird-animal-Universe. Every shaman had his special attributes—tambourine and drum, and depictions of the spirit-helpers. These depictions were made of wood and stood in the shaman's dwelling, or were used as pendants in the costume.

In addition to shamanism, Siberian people had many religious beliefs, expressed in organized cults. The attributes of these cults were the spirit-helpers, guardians of house and hearth, often depicted in anthropomorphic and zoomorphic forms.

OVERCOAT

91 cm high

Seal guts

SIBERIA, Eskimo

19th century

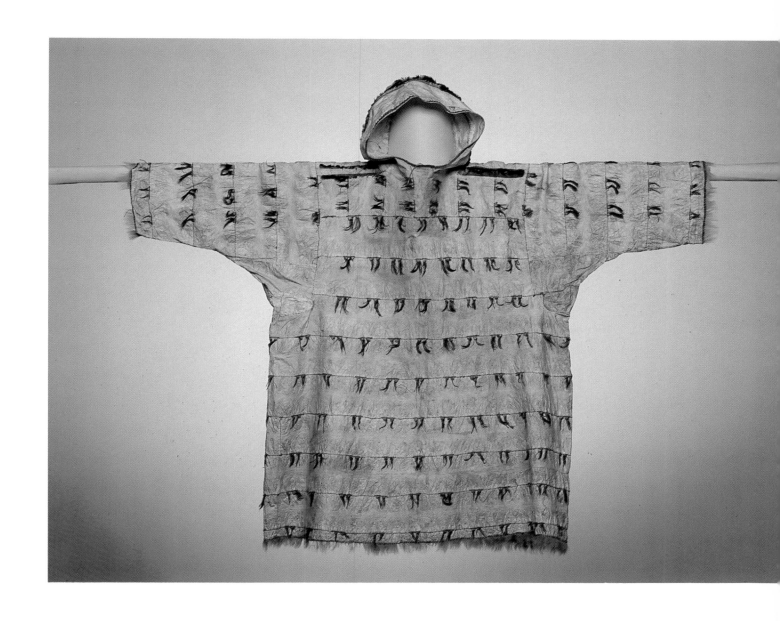

In the 18th century, Lomonosov, a famous Russian scientist, wrote that the richness and glory of Russia will grow from Siberia. These words appeared to be prophetic, and now Siberia is known not only for gold, coal and oil, but is a shining star of folk art which has spread all over the world, enriching the lives of many different people. The creations of the Siberian people have taken their rightful place in the world of the 20th century.

SHAMAN'S COSTUME

Suede, metal, textile

SIBERIA, Evenks

19th century

SHAMAN'S TIGER
For protection from diseases

74 cm long
Wood

SIBERIA, Nanai
19th century

164

Major Donors to Mingei International

INDIVIDUALS
Margaret Barlow
Norma Djerassi
Sidney and Eve Gulick
Jean and Ernest Hahn
Alan and Nora Jaffe
Sydney Martin Roth
Anna M. Saulsbery
Millard & Mary Sheets
Mr. and Mrs. Worley W. Stewart
Rosemary Braun Utecht

FOUNDATIONS
Ahmanson Foundation
The Seymour E. Clonick Memorial Fund
The James S. Copley Foundation
The Drown Foundation
The Favrot Fund
The James Irvine Foundation
The Kerr Foundation
The Knight Aid Fund
Las Patronas
The Gerald and Inez Grant Parker Foundation
The Robert Peterson Foundation
The Roth Fund
The Skaggs Foundation

CORPORATIONS
Bazaar del Mundo
California First Bank
The Flour Corporation
University Towne Centre Associates
The Hahn Company
JMB Realty
Mervyn's
San Diego Gas and Electric

GOVERNMENT AGENCIES
California Arts Council
The City of San Diego
The County of San Diego
Institute of Museum Services
The National Endowment for the Arts
COMBO

Exhibition Production

MARTHA LONGENECKER, design
JOANNE HEANEY, co-designer
ROBERTA SHAW, consultant
DEAN CONGER, photographs for murals
  (courtesy of National Geographic Society)
AL GOODMAN and
MARSHALL WISEMAN, electrical
JULIAN FRANK, lighting
ELLIOT RABIN, plastics
CHARLES HOUCHIN, Lutes Cabinets
DOROTHY D. STEWART and
LINDA TEAGUE, floral arrangements
MR. and MRS. ERNEST W. HAHN, reception chairmen

Publication

MARTHA LONGENECKER, design and editing
LYNTON GARDINER, photography
MOOG AND ASSOCIATES INC., typesetting and
  art production
SPRING COLOR, color separations
  Rep. Tim Gallagher
VANARD LITHOGRAPHY, printing

Production Assistants

VICTOR ARREOLA
NORA JAFFE
ANNE O'BRIEN
ANNA SAULSBERY
MARY ANN SMITH